A GUIDE TO
SUNSET CRATER
AND WUPATKI

WRITTEN BY SCOTT THYBONY

PHOTOGRAPHY BY GEORGE H.H. HUEY

■

WESTERN NATIONAL PARKS ASSOCIATION

TUCSON, ARIZONA

After flourishing for over a century, prehistoric Indians abandoned their pueblos leaving behind a landscape of ruins.

A VISITOR AT WUPATKI wrote in the register that he'd never seen such wide open spaces. On the line below his comment a visiting Russian added, "We have even better—Siberia."

There may be more stretch to Siberia, but the quality of space surrounding Sunset Crater and Wupatki is unique. It's not only wide open, spreading horizontally along the course of the Little Colorado River, but high open—dropping vertically from the mountains at Sunset Crater to the desert at Wupatki. The light filtering through the ancient blue sky falls over a geology so fresh it looks hot to the touch and ruins so well-preserved that time takes a turn and we find ourselves moving closer to the past.

We are entrusted with preserving this remarkable place so that we can return time after time to discover new aspects of its natural and cultural beauty.

Each section of the guidebook is self-contained so that a visitor can use it traveling either direction. Those starting at the north entrance can turn to the back and follow the guide in reverse order.

The guidebook begins at the south entrance turnoff to Sunset Crater National Monument on Highway 89. It then follows the Sunset Crater/Wupatki road as it curves past Sunset Crater (4 miles), drops into the desert near the Wupatki Ruins (21.5 miles) and rejoins Highway 89 at the north entrance (35.3 miles).

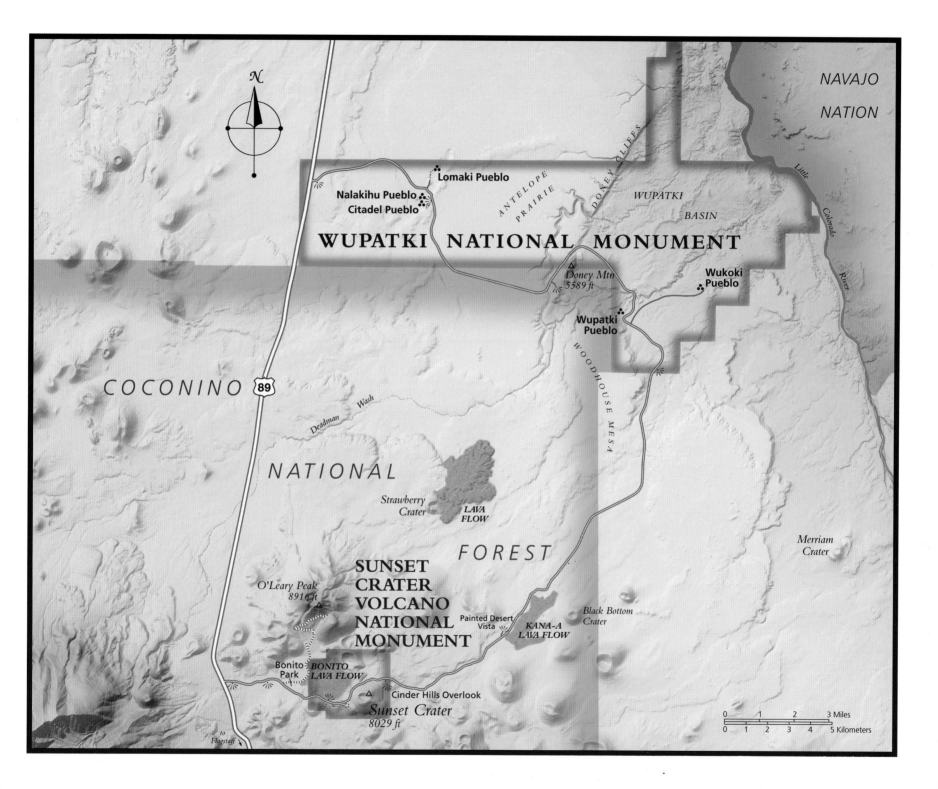

NAVAJO NATION

Lomaki Pueblo

Nalakihu Pueblo
Citadel Pueblo

ANTELOPE PRAIRIE

DONEY CLIFFS

WUPATKI BASIN

WUPATKI NATIONAL MONUMENT

Doney Mtn
5589 ft

Wukoki Pueblo

Wupatki Pueblo

COCONINO

89

Deadman Wash

WOODHOUSE MESA

NATIONAL

Strawberry Crater

LAVA FLOW

Merriam Crater

FOREST

SUNSET CRATER VOLCANO NATIONAL MONUMENT

O'Leary Peak
8916 ft

Painted Desert Vista

KANA-A LAVA FLOW

Black Bottom Crater

Bonito Park

BONITO LAVA FLOW

Cinder Hills Overlook

Sunset Crater
8029 ft

to Flagstaff

Little Colorado River

0   1   2   3 Miles

0   1   2   3   4   5 Kilometers

SACRED MOUNTAINS. The San Francisco Peaks dominate the skyline to the west. Rising from the surrounding desert, yet snow covered for much of the year, they reflect the contrasts of the landscape. Seen from the Indian country to the north, the high peaks seem to generate their own weather, giving birth to clouds which drift across the Painted Desert bringing rain to the Navajo and Hopi lands. The peaks are sacred to the Indians who occasionally make pilgrimages to place prayer feathers at shrines high in the mountains. Hopi and Navajo medicine men have joined forces in the past to prevent recreational development on the mountain. The summits are now protected in the Kachina Peaks Wilderness Area.

Reaching 12,633 feet, the peaks are the highest in Arizona, although they are only remnants of a much larger volcanic mountain estimated to have reached 15,000 feet. The summit of the ancestral peak collapsed into the empty magma chamber 500,000 years ago. The result was a series of peaks surrounding an inner basin that was further enlarged by the grinding of glaciers during the ice ages. Alluvial deposits, partially from glacial outwash, cover much of the area.

The volcanic field surrounding the San Francisco Peaks is one of the largest in the country. Eruptions over the last two million years have covered more than 2200 square miles with ashfall and lava flows. Scientists are intrigued by the possibility of a cyclic pattern to these eruptions but speculation outweighs any proof. The U.S. Geological Survey has ranked the San Franicsco volcanic field near the bottom of a list of thirty-five sites in the United States most likely to erupt.

The Hopi still leave prayer sticks at shrines hidden on the mountain summits and within the broken lava flows.

BONITO PARK
Elevation: 7010 feet

POTSHERDS AND PALETTES. The surprising discovery that man had lived at Sunset Crater at the time of the eruption began with a watercolor painted in Bonito Park. In 1930, Major Lionel F. Brady, a geologist with the Museum of Northern Arizona, was asked to accompany a visiting artist to Sunset Crater. The easel was set up at a choice view point in Bonito Park, and the artist began to paint. With nothing to do, Brady began poking around the cinders and noticed a few scattered potsherds that looked old. He stuck these in a pocket of his baggy field pants and later showed them to Harold S. Colton, the museum director.

Colton was excited. They were earlier than anything found before in the area and might predate the ashfall. Colton soon had his crew excavate a trench where the potsherds had been found. After cutting through deep layers of volcanic ash, they reached a buried pit house. People undoubtedly had been living here when the crater erupted, and it was now obvious that Sunset Crater had formed more recently than anyone had suspected.

Stimulated by these new finds, Colton began an intensive effort to archeologically date the eruption. Extensive excavations were undertaken in Bonito Park and the Medicine Valley area to the north during the next two summers. Ceramic evidence and tree-ring dating, then a new science, indicated an eruption between A.D. 875 and 910. Over the years a number of adjustments were made to this date as new evidence accumulated. When corings were taken from beams used to build the Wupatki pueblo, the tree rings showed there had been several years of stunted growth, probably caused by hot ashes damaging the trees. This information led scientists to date the primary eruption at sometime between the fall of A.D. 1064 and the spring of 1065.

Western bluebirds, winter visitors to the monument, find a perch on a dried mullein stalk.

Penstemon (right) *and other wildflowers now grow where the Sinagua once raised corn and beans.*

7

The devastating effects of the eruption of Sunset Crater are recorded in these narrow growth rings. Tree rings helped accurately date the birth of the volcano between fall 1064 and spring 1065.

8

THE WATERLESS MOUNTAINS. Colton named the prehistoric Indians living in the area at the time of the eruption the "Sinagua" (Spanish for "without water") after an early name for the San Francisco Peaks. The Sinagua lived in small, pit house villages in the ponderosa pine forest on the edge of open parks. They had been growing crops in Bonito Park for several centuries, consequently the soil had become depleted. Some had already begun farming more marginal lands, even before the eruption of Sunset Crater.

Throughout the forest are open parks similar to Bonito Park. These are formed by clay deposits near the surface that prevent drainage. In some cases there is too much drainage caused by cinders and the porous nature of the underlying limestone.

North of Bonito Park is O'Leary Peak, named after Dan O'Leary, a guide for General George Crook during the Indian wars. The peak is formed of volcanic domes similar to those which have formed in Mount St. Helen's crater. The major eruption of O'Leary Peak happened 230,000 years ago.

East of Bonito Park are the Bonito Campground, which is closed during winter, and the Sunset Crater Visitor Center. An earthquake monitoring system in the visitor center is sensitive enough to detect major earthquakes from around the world. Most local earthquake activity is thought to be caused by underlying volcanic movements.

Major Lionel F. Brady.   *Harold S. Colton.*

Desert and forest meet—a prickly-pear cactus blooms in a bed of ponderosa pine needles.

9

BONITO LAVA FLOW
Elevation: 6960 feet

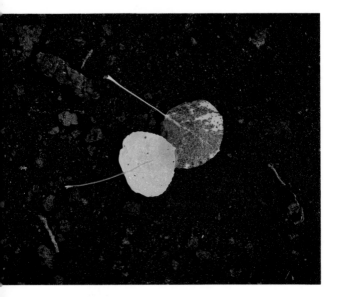

RIVER OF STONE. Bonito Lava Flow is a geologic snapshot, a burning river of jagged lava that has been stopped motionless in time. The hardened flow of lava bears witness to the deep forces of the earth that are at once destructive and creative.

Bonito Flow was unable to find an outlet in the surrounding cinder cones when it squeezed from the base of Sunset Crater. Instead it pooled up, reaching a depth of 100 feet in some places. As the lava flowed it cooled very quickly where it made contact with the air or the underlying earth, forming a hard shell around the still molten interior. Inside the lava continued to flow slowly. Lava tubes formed whenever the lava drained from the shell of hardened lava. Other caves in the flow are formed by fissures. Both types are known locally as ice caves, since ice can form in them and last year round. In fact, they contained so much ice in the late 1880s that they supplied not only local homesteaders but also the Flagstaff saloons.

A short trail enters the lava flow at the Bonito Lava Flow pullout providing a close-up look at the jagged formation. The rough, churned surface formed as the cooling rubble rode on a slowly advancing core of molten lava. Occasionally the brittle outer shell of the flow would crack deep enough for the molten interior to ooze to the surface, forming squeeze-ups. Volcanic gases escaped through cone-shaped vents called fumaroles. Upon contact with the air and surrounding rock, these gases formed brightly colored deposits around the vent.

LUNAR LANDSCAPE. Although Bonito Flow pushed from the base of Sunset Crater over 700 years ago, it appears to have cooled yesterday. Like the pitted surface of the moon, this land on the edge of the desert wears its scars a long time.

During the 1960s NASA worked frantically to put a man on the moon. As the Apollo astronauts underwent intensive training, there was a need for hands-on experience in terrain similar to what they would find on the moon. The Sunset Crater region was a natural choice. A plywood mock-up of a lunar module was built on the north side of the lava flow. Craters were blasted in cinder fields south of the monument to simulate the Sea of Tranquility, the landing site for Apollo 11. A mock lunar rover called "Grover" toured the crater field. Wearing cumbersome spacesuits, the astronauts lumbered over the cinder hills collecting rock samples and getting a feel for life in an alien environment. Neil Armstrong, the first man to set foot on the moon, was among the many astronauts who trained here.

The primal tangle of black rock is an ideal environment for training astronauts, but a less than encouraging one for the growth of plants. Yet the green of a twisted ponderosa pine struggling to grow from the black lava flow shows that the scarred landscape is slowly healing. In a tropical region like Hawaii it's only a matter of years before the jungle returns. In

Lava flowing from the base of Sunset Crater created a jagged river of stone—ideal for training astronauts, but less than encouraging for this aspen.

the desert Southwest it takes centuries for the land to come alive again.

The first sign of life to appear on the cooled rocks is an odd crusty growth called a lichen. Although inconspicuous, it is an extremely important step in establishing life on the bare rock. The lichen secretes a weak acid which disintegrates rock and forms the soil necessary for other plants to take root. The lichen exists because of an unusual organic partnership. It is actually two plants, an alga and fungus, neither of which could survive on its own in the environments where the lichen thrives. The algae contain chlorophyll and produce food which they share with the fungi. The fungi, in turn, provide the shelter that protects and retains moisture, most of which is absorbed from the air. These unassuming plants may live several hundred years, and colonies may survive for thousands of years. Even on such harsh terrain as a lava flow, life is tenacious and persistent.

After lichen establishes a foothold, the succession of plants begins to accelerate. Mosses trap dust and water from the air and form a rich soil for seed plants. At first the annuals take hold, then the perennials. Eventually enough soil is formed for trees to take root, but at Sunset Crater the process is slow. A few struggling ponderosa have taken root on the flow where winds have deposited soil. Several more centuries will pass before the pine forest will cover the land devastated by the eruption. Most of the ponderosa in the monument are less than a hundred years old and are often stunted and deformed by a lack of water and strong winds.

Shallow roots of a stunted ponderosa pine struggle to find enough moisture to survive on Bonito Lava Flow (left).

An aspen grows straight and tall in the deep ash on the edge of the lava flow (above).

Looking more volcanic than organic, the rough-skinned horned toad feeds almost exclusively on red ants.

SUNSET CRATER

Elevation: 6960 feet (*base*), 8030 feet (*rim*)

THE SMOKING EARTH. It was dark when a geologist reached the Mexican village of Paricutín after a hurried trip. He had received reports of a volcanic eruption and although skeptical, had rushed to the scene. That night, in 1943, Dr. Ezequiel Ordóñez saw and heard what few have witnessed, the birth of a volcano almost a twin of Sunset Crater.

"Tremendous explosions were heard, ground tremors were felt frequently, and a thick high column of vapors with a great many incandescent rocks could be seen rising almost continuously from the center of a small conical mound . . .," he wrote, ". . . at times a 'chugging' noise like that of a starting locomotive was heard."

The volcano Dr. Ordóñez watched had begun to form two days before in a freshly plowed cornfield. The farmer noticed the ground was unusually warm and a light trace of smoke was seeping from a small crack. Within a matter of months the cinder cone had grown over 1000 feet.

Sunset Crater is the youngest of over 400 volcanoes found in the San Francisco volcanic field, and looks remarkably similar to the volcano which began in the farmer's field near Paricutín. Sunset Crater erupted as William of Normandy was preparing to invade England, and it is just possible that it, too, began in the middle of a cornfield. The valley where Sunset Crater formed was being farmed by the local Indians.

Most eruptions are preceded by earthquakes, so the Sinagua Indians may have had enough warning of the impending erup- tion to gather their belongings and leave the area. Excavated pit houses that were buried under ash from the eruption have turned up very little in the way of possessions. In some pit houses even the roof beams and posts were removed.

When the eruption did occur, though, it may have been extremely violent. Magma is gas-rich lava held inside the earth under tremendous pressure. When this pressure is suddenly released, the gas separates explosively from the magma. The eruption of Mount St. Helens was so violent that a 1000-foot section of the mountain was blown off in the first ten minutes. Although Sunset Crater's eruption may not have been as explosive, a tremendous amount of material was ejected from the cinder cone. Winds from the southwest deposited ash and cinders over 800 square miles.

In 1975 Dr. Eugene Shoemaker of the U.S. Geological Survey began to date the ashfalls and flows of Sunset Crater using paleomagnetic techniques. He found that the earlier tree-ring dates for the initial ash and cinder eruption that formed most of the cinder cone were essentially correct. The eruption of Sunset Crater began sometime after September 1064 and before June 1065.

Ash and cinder eruptions continued for a few decades forming most of the existing cinder cone. After a short, quiet period, the Kana´a Lava Flow erupted from the base of the young cinder cone about 1065 and flowed east, followed thirty years later by several eruptions of ash, cinder and lava bombs. Then in 1180 Bonito Lava Flow emerged. Ash and cinder continued to erupt sporadically until all activity ended about 1220 when the dying volcano spewed red cinders along the crest of the crater.

Sunset Crater, composed primarily of dark gray, unconsolidated cinders, rises 1000 feet above Bonito Flow. Red cinders form the rim, giving the cinder cone a fiery, glowing appearance. In the crater itself are additional deposits of yellow, purple and green. In their descriptive way of naming, the Navajo call this the "Yellow-topped Mountain," while the Hopi call it "Red Hill." The actual crater drops 400 feet into the top of the cinder cone and is best seen from the fire lookout road that meanders up the side of O'Leary Peak.

SPECIAL EFFECTS. One of the first geologists to be impressed by the beauty and symmetry of Sunset Crater was

The 1943 eruption of Paricutín (left) created a cinder cone almost identical to Sunset Crater.

Cinders spewed along the rim of Sunset Crater during the final eruption causing its reddish glow; a Sinagua plainware jar reflects this warm color (left).

17

John Wesley Powell. He first saw the mountain in 1892 when he was the director of the U.S. Geological Survey. "On viewing the mountain from a distance," he wrote, "the red cinders seem to be on fire . . . the peak seems to glow with a light of its own." He called this colorful volcano, Sunset Peak, a name that park rangers wish had stuck. Visitors to the monument have been known to drive right past Sunset Crater without seeing it, thinking a crater should be a hole in the ground and not one on top of a mountain.

Early travelers to Sunset Crater had their work cut out for them. Grace Spradling recorded a climb she made in 1917. "Well its [sic] one of the queerest trails you ever saw for the whole mt [sic] is nothing but cinders," she wrote in her diary. "The trail goes nearly straight up the side of mt. and the cinders make it so you take 3 steps up & slide back 2." Because the cinders are so loose, decades of hikers taking three steps up and two back had seriously scarred the sides of the mountain. In the early 1970s it was closed to hikers, but an easy mile-long trail now loops through the lava flow at the base of the mountain. The Lava Flow Nature Trail passes squeeze-ups, fumaroles and clinkers that look so fresh you stop and listen for the hiss, spatter and ooze of the lava.

In 1928 a Hollywood film company planned to dynamite the slopes of Sunset Crater to create what they hoped would be a spectacular landslide. Word of their planned special effects leaked out. Angry protests from the people of Flagstaff prevented this needless destruction, and once the immediate crisis was over they realized that long-term protection was needed. Encouraged by a strong lobbying effort, President Hoover set aside Sunset Crater as a national monument in 1930.

Flannel mullein often seen along the road can reach heights of six feet.

18

Rabbitbrush brightens the cinder slopes of Sunset Crater. The fringe of trees along the misty crest remind the Hopi of dancing Kachinas.

CINDER HILLS
Elevation: 7060 feet

A young plant erupts where rivers of molten rock once flowed.

BLACK RAIN. Gyp Crater and a series of red spatter cones, seen from the Cinder Hills Overlook, were formed by spectacular fire fountains erupting for miles along a fissure. This event occurred during the last phase of the Sunset Crater eruptions.

A natural event of such magnitude must have had a profound effect on the Sinagua Indians who were living here. What must have seemed to them an unparalleled disaster, or if the Hopi myths provide a clue, an act of divine retribution, actually contained the seeds of hope. The ash that fell at the edge of their homeland would eventually revitalize their flagging agriculture. While Sunset Crater was still active, the Sinagua began to move from the high country into the pinyon–juniper forest and desert grasslands at the edge of the ashfall. This movement was at first tentative, probing. As their new fields yielded good crops, more and more families joined those who had already settled.

Along the margins of the ashfall where the cinders were not too deep, the Sinagua discovered crops could be dry-farmed in areas never before used for farming. Seeds were planted in virgin soils covered by dark ash that absorbed the sunlight and may have extended the growing season. Most importantly, it provided a mulch. The fine cinders absorbed and held the sporadic rains and winter snows for longer periods than the native soil. Experiments have shown that cinder cover does help corn to germinate and grow. And the beneficial effect on plant life is reflected in the distribution of trees. Because of the cinders, ponderosa pine and aspen are found 1000 feet below their normal range.

As the Sinagua moved into the black sand country northeast of the volcano, they came into closer contact with neighboring tribes, taking the best from their ways of life and making it their own. Their population increased, large ceremonial centers emerged, vast new areas were opened to farming and trade networks expanded. During the 200 years that Sunset

Crater continued to erupt their culture reached a new level of complexity.

The eruption of Sunset Crater was such a dramatic event it's natural to give it credit for the great social developments that occurred. But often it's the quiet, subtle shifts in nature that trigger the greatest changes. This may have been the case with the Sinagua. Although the ashfall seems to have been an important factor in drawing them down from the mountain, there was also a slight increase in summer rainfall that began at this time throughout the Southwest. More rain may have been the key factor that allowed crops to be dry-farmed on the edge of the desert. Evidence for increased rainfall comes from tree-ring studies and the fact that in many post-eruption sites the bones of geese, ducks and cranes are found in greater numbers.

Across the Painted Desert some Hopi villages were settled while Sunset Crater was still active. The Hopi people are still there, and it seems likely that an eye-witness account of so dramatic an event might be found in their oral traditions. One story is a good candidate. Among the legends recorded by early ethnographers is an account of the destruction of a corrupt village by clouds of ash. The people of this Hopi village were told of an unusual light seen on the mountain that was beginning to spread toward them. Most ignored the warnings and continued to gamble in the kivas, although a few good people listened and left in time. Soon a large cloud of ash swept over the village destroying all who remained.

A common theme threads its way through many Hopi stories. Disaster and destruction come not when times are hard and the people are struggling. They come in times of prosperity when the people have been corrupted by the material world and fail to perform their religious duties.

WIND GOD AND WATERFALL. While no hard evidence has been found to link the Hopi story with the final eruption, the Sunset Crater region still holds a special significance for the Hopi. The crater itself is said to be the home of the friendly Kana´a Kachinas. The stunted trees on the summit of the crater look to the Hopi like their holy kachina spirits dancing along the rim. The wind god, Yaponcha, is said to live in a deep fissure at the base of the cinder cone. Once when the winds had grown very destructive, the Twin War Gods sealed Yaponcha in his home. This caused hot weather and a drought, so they had to return and open a small hole to let out just the right amount of wind. On rare occasions the Hopi still leave prayer feathers at shrines near Sunset Crater.

Farther to the southeast on the edge of the cinder hills is Merriam Crater where lava once flowed into the Little Colorado River, damming the channel and diverting the river over the canyon wall downstream. This formed Grand Falls, and when the river is in flood, a spectacular waterfall, the color of frothy Mexican chocolate, plunges 185 feet.

This carved kachina doll represents the friendly Kana´a spirit that the Hopi believe live on Sunset Crater.

PAINTED DESERT VISTA
Elevation: 6280 feet

PAINTED ROCK, STONE TREES AND DINOSAURS.
Shimmering in the far distance across the Little Colorado
River lies the Painted Desert. The intense sun at midday
bleaches the landscape to a monotonous gray-brown. Yet in the
morning and evening or when storm clouds are gathering a
transformation occurs. The desert becomes iridescent.
Multiple shades of red, blue and purple bleed from the rock
with an intensity that always surprises.

The Painted Desert was independently named by both
Spanish and American explorers—a name so well known yet a
place so seldom visited. The most familiar section is Petrified
Forest National Park, but the dune fields, eroded escarpments
and colorful desolation stretch for hundreds of miles.

Although most famous for its petrified wood, the Painted
Desert is rich in dinosaur and early mammal fossils. Over the
years numerous expeditions have searched here for clues to the
evolution of life. The fossil beds have yielded bones of one of the
oldest dinosaurs and one of the oldest mammals, a shrew-like
creature that lived during the age of the dinosaurs 180 million
years ago.

LIFE ZONES AND THIRST ZONES. The distance
between the Little Colorado River and the top of the San
Francisco Peaks is less than thirty miles, yet the elevation
changes dramatically. A gain of 8000 feet in so short a distance
attracted the famous biologist, C. Hart Merriam, to investigate
the way animal and plant communities change with elevation.

In 1889, Merriam and his small party crossed the Little
Colorado River. They wandered in the Painted Desert for three
days, unable to find water. They were rescued in the nick of
time by an old Hopi who guided them to a muddy seep. He
stuck a rubber hose into the mud and began sucking. When he
had a mouthful he would spit it into an old pot that he finally
offered to the thirsty party. Merriam accepted the gift, but first

threw in a handful of coffee grounds, then boiled it.

The result of Merriam's study was his theory of Life Zones.
He believed the distribution of plants and animals on a mountain duplicated vertically, in a short distance, what might be
found horizontally over 1000 miles from the deserts of Mexico
to the Canadian arctic. The highest zone was the Arctic-alpine
followed by the Hudsonian, Canadian and Transition zones.
The two desert zones were the Upper Sonoran and the Lower
Sonoran. All but the last are found in the vicinity of the peaks.
That so many life zones are found so close together may be
another factor why the prehistoric Indians chose to live here.
When the harvest was poor they could gather wild plants and
hunt. The diversity of plants and animals and the way plants at
different elevations ripen at different times of the year would
contribute to the Indians' survival.

On the far side of the Painted Desert are the Hopi Mesas.
Some of the Sinagua who left the Wupatki area may have
merged with the ancestors of the Hopi. A walk through one of
the Hopi villages today shows obvious similarities to the
prehistoric peoples of the Wupatki region—house styles,
methods of farming, tools. Another possible connection is a
story told by a Hopi who spent several seasons helping to
excavate the ruins of Wupatki. He said that another Hopi once
asked him if he remembered anyone finding a man buried with
a dog and parrots. The question surprised him because they
had excavated just such a burial. The curious Hopi said
members of his clan still remembered the buried man's name.
He was a chief called Chipiya.

THE CAMOUFLAGED DESERT. Within a short distance
of the Little Colorado River the desert scrub gives way to
grasslands. As elevation increases south of Wupatki a few
scattered junipers begin to appear like sentinels of the pinyon–
juniper forest. But even when the forest is reached and

The pinyon pine gives shelter in winter and shade in summer to many animals, like the coyote (right), *that make their home in the pinyon-juniper life zone.*

Fragrant flowers of the primrose appear in early evening and wilt by morning .

treecover is thick, the land is still extremely arid. The lack of surface water turns the forest into a desert with trees.

The dry pinyon–juniper forest provides a habitat for many kinds of wildlife. One of the more familiar is the coyote *(Canis latrans)*. Although most active at night, it is occasionally seen trotting over the horizon or resting in the shade of a juniper during the day. Coyotes rarely travel in groups of more than two or three, although their wide range of howls and yips can sound like a raucous coyote convention, especially if you happen to be camped nearby.

Bobcats *(Lynx rufus)* also range through the forest, and since they hunt primarily at night they have developed an acute sense of hearing. Their long ear tufts probably help by directing sound waves to the ear. Large ear spots mimic eyes that give the impression of a larger, more fierce head. These spots also serve as visual cues to help the kittens follow their mother. One of the bobcats' favorite meals is the packrat *(Neotoma albigula)*. The packrat has a reputation as a thief with a conscience since it takes items from unwary campers but always leaves something in return. It seems the packrat has an obsessive interest in shiny objects and will drop whatever it's carrying—a twig or a cactus needle—and pick up the shiny object. The exchange is probably unintentional.

Northwest of the Painted Desert Vista is the Strawberry Crater Wilderness Area, managed by the U.S. Forest Service. Northeast across the highway is Black Bottom Crater and the Kana´a Lava Flow. This flow was the first to erupt from the base of Sunset Crater and poured down Kana´a Wash for six miles. Subsequent cinder and ash eruptions covered much of it.

WUKOKI
Elevation: 4600 feet

RAVEN'S WATCH. In the off-season a raven often perches on the rim of Wukoki Ruin surveying the silence. It rests high on a wall so well preserved that many visitors think it has been restored. When a car drives up, the raven flies off for another quiet perch. Some of those who walk over from their cars pass quickly through the ruins and return before the raven is out of sight. But others stand in awe, taking up the raven's watch.

What perennial fascination do ruins hold for people? Perhaps it's a recognition that we ultimately share the same fate. What this fate is we are left to guess. Some may see the striking ruins of Wukoki as a failure. Others may find it remarkable that the prehistoric Indians came to live here in the first place and made the attempt to understand this land and bend it to their own use.

After 800 years, the winds and rains have stripped Wukoki, exposing the underlying stone structure. Built on an island of red Moenkopi sandstone surrounded by a wash of black cinders, the walls of dressed rock rise three stories. Where wall begins and bedrock ends is hard to tell; the ruins seem to grow from the rock itself.

The architecture blends perfectly with the environment of the Wupatki Basin. This may be as much an accident of time as purposeful design. The walls, both inside and out, were probably plastered and may have had designs painted on them. If these walls were not meant to be seen then why go to the trouble to make them aesthetically pleasing? A number of ruins in the area are banded with different colored rock. If there was a meaning behind these patterns it has been lost. What remains is a particular approach to the world. The prehistoric Indians seem to have been expressing an attitude that the unseen was as important to them as the seen when they built a beautiful wall only to cover it with plaster.

The Moenkopi sandstones and siltstones used to build Wukoki were deposited over 200 million years ago when the terrain was covered by either a broad river or mud flats periodically swept by a shallow sea. Ripple marks from the water currents are often found on the rock, and mud cracks show that drying occasionally took place. Although rare, the tracks of a primitive reptile, *Chirotherium,* are found in the Moenkopi. The tracks of these five-toed creatures puzzled early observers. The thumbs looked as if they were on the outside instead of the inside, giving rise to the tongue-in-cheek theory that they must have walked like a cross-legged frog. It was later noted that the "thumb" was actually an oversized little finger.

SCIENTISTS, SOLDIERS AND INDIANS. Probing westward from the Little Colorado in 1851, Lt. Lorenzo Sitgreaves commanded a party searching for a practical route across northern Arizona. As they began the climb away from the river, probably following an old Indian trail, they found themselves among a landscape of ruins. Sitgreaves saw broken pottery everywhere and found "all the prominent points occupied by the ruins of stone houses of considerable size, and in some instances, of three stories in height." But there was no sign of anyone still occupying this dry country. These houses had been abandoned, he believed, because of the lack of water.

In 1896 Ben Doney guided the archeologist, Dr. Jesse W. Fewkes, through the Wupatki Basin. Fewkes undertook the first scientific reconnaissance of the area, photographing, mapping and describing most of the major ruins. He also excavated a sandstone crypt containing a woman buried with many pieces of fine pottery and well-crafted ear pendants that were covered with turquoise mosaics. Fewkes estimated that Wukoki had been lived in by one or two families for several generations. A Hopi Snake Clan legend claims it was a

Wukoki Ruin is an island of red sandstone surrounded by a wash of black cinders.

26

Witness to centuries of summer storms, Wukoki
still stands like a fortress.

28

stopping place for their people after they left their home near Navajo Mountain.

When the early scientists began studying the ancient ruins, Navajo Indians were still living in the Wupatki Basin. The nomadic Navajo may have camped along the Little Colorado River as early as the 1820s. They remained highly mobile until defeated by the U.S. Army under Kit Carson in the 1860s and forcibly removed to New Mexico. Some settled permanently in the Wupatki Basin when they returned from captivity. Peshlakai Atsidi was the local headman who made two trips to Washington to represent his people in disputes with local ranchers. Once Peshlakai had to deal with a white man who had no understanding of Navajo customs. Overlooking a breach of etiquette by the newcomer, Peshlakai remarked, "What can you expect from a tribe which has only one god and then swears by his name?"

When Peshlakai's wife was troubled by dreams and periods of sickness she called in a medicine man to find out what was wrong. He told her that the spirits of the dead Indians that the archeologists were then beginning to dig up had entered her body. So she had him perform a ceremony to drive them out.

In recent times the grandmother of a young Navajo who worked at the monument came and took the girl away. The concerned grandmother thought she worked too close to the ruins for her own good. Over 160 Navajo sites have been recorded in the monument. Some of these are burial hogans known as *hokai*, or "fear hogans." A few of Peshlakai's descendents still live in the area.

Navajo headman Peshlakai Atsidi and his son, Clyde, 1920.

It is thought the Sinagua may have learned how to build large pueblos from the neighboring Anasazi. Black on white potsherds echo the Anasazi influence.

29

WUPATKI

Elevation: 4810 feet

BLACK SAND COUNTRY. While the natural landscape reshaped itself with periodic eruptions, the Sinagua Indians began to reshape their own cultural landscape. They came out of their earth-covered homes and down from the high country. In the desert along Deadman's Wash they began to construct towering stone villages that could house over a hundred people.

From what remains, we can see that construction of this magnitude took a great deal of technological sophistication. Skills in planning, engineering and stone masonry are apparent. Where did the Sinagua learn these skills? Stone was used in some of their pit houses, but nothing approaching the sophisticated stonework found at Wupatki. The most likely source was the Anasazi, who were also living in the Wupatki Basin and had been building stone pueblos for some time. Whatever the source, the Sinagua learned quickly and incorporated their new knowledge into their on-going way of life.

The prehistoric ruins of Wupatki are located on the edge of the black sand country. The area is rich in archeology but short on water. Wupatki itself was built next to one of the few permanent springs, and the people who lived here exploited every available source of water, even setting pots at the edge of overhanging rocks to catch the run-off. The Indians relied on rainfall to water their crops. Today this land is used only for grazing.

TALL HOUSE. Wupatki is the largest ruin in the region, but the period of dynamic growth it represents was short-lived. Major building on the pueblo began about A.D. 1120 with the population peaking about fifty years later. The pueblo reached four stories, may have contained up to 100 rooms—many of which have not been excavated—and was occupied by about 125 people. Construction ended in 1195, and over the next

Wupatki Pueblo's finely crafted masonry walls once housed over a hundred people.

Common resident of the Wupatki Basin, Apache-plume is named for its striking feathery seed pods.

twenty years Wupatki was gradually abandoned.

Near the pueblo is the Wupatki Ball Court, enclosed by a banked stone wall. We do not know what game the Indians played here, but it probably resembled the highly ritualized game played by the Aztecs and Mayans in similar courts, using rubber balls identical to those found in Arizona. When the early Spanish saw this game they were surprised by its speed and ferocity. The players would try to keep the ball in the air without using their hands or feet. Heads, elbows, and hips were allowed. The object of the game was to knock the ball through a stone ring, ending the game. But before the winning point could be scored the game would sometimes last for days. In Mesoamerica, the desire to win was no doubt high since those who lost were sometimes sacrificed. There is no evidence, though, that losers were sacrificed in the south-western United States.

Not far from the ballcourt is another unusual feature—the blow hole. Other blow holes are found throughout the monument and seem to be connected to a large system of underground fissures. Acting as a natural barometer, air blows out at speeds up to thirty-five miles per hour when the atmospheric pressure is low; when it is high, the stream of air reverses and flows into the earth. Blow holes seem to have held a special significance for the Indians of Wupatki. Many large pueblos are built near them, and even today one is used by Navajo medicine men for curing ceremonies.

The abandonment of the Wupatki Basin is now seen as a reversal of those trends that allowed the people to live here in the first place. The rains began to lessen, the growing season may have shortened as the climate cooled, winds blew away the valuable ash, and the soil itself may have become depleted. However, the Indians had survived periods of extreme environmental stress before, so the mystery of why they left still remains.

After Wupatki was deserted, a small group of Hopi may have occupied the pueblo for a short time. A few broken pieces of their pottery were found during excavations, and they claim that members of the Parrot Clan are buried here. After the Hopi left there is no evidence of anyone living here until the 1880s when sheepherders cleared the rubble from two rooms at Wupatki to use for their camp. During this period occasional pothunters and, more rarely, a visiting scientist would use the ruins. Eventually a bootlegger set up operations. He must have thought the spot ideal because of its isolation, but it had one drawback—no wood to fire his still. Undaunted, his solution was to use the ancient roof beams from the ruins.

The increasing destruction prompted those who were concerned with the beauty and archeological value of the

The now silent ballcourt at Wupatki was once the setting for a game thought to be as vigorous and grueling as one played in similar ballcourts in Mexico.

region to call for protection. This eventually resulted in a proclamation issued by President Calvin Coolidge in 1924 that established Wupatki National Monument. One of the citizens most active in creating the monument was J.C. Clarke who was appointed the first custodian. The position was largely honorary since he was paid the salary of only $1 a year. It wasn't until 1934 that a full-time ranger was hired.

At first the ranger took up housekeeping in the ruins themselves, but as visitors to the monument increased, he decided to build a separate house nearby. During the construction of the ranger's new home, a local Navajo realized he also needed a new house and set to work. When the ranger saw the improvised walls of scrap metal and junk wood, he sat down and had a talk with his friend. The ranger tried his best to sell the Navajo on all the benefits of the traditional Navajo hogan. Finally the Navajo asked, "You like old hogan better than new house?"

"I certainly do," answered the ranger, "very much better."

"That's fine!" exclaimed the Indian. "You move into hogan, I move into new ranger house. Everybody happy."

Another type of switch happened years before. As map makers know, place names have a perverse way of drifting across the map from feature to feature. The Wupatki and Wukoki ruins were given their Hopi names by Dr. Jesse W. Fewkes. Wupatki roughly translates as "tall house" and was originally applied to the Wukoki ruins. Wukoki means "big and wide house," a name which Fewkes originally gave to the large ruin near the visitor center. When the monument was established, the names had been switched somehow and were in wide use. To change back, it was believed, would have invited even greater confusion.

Whether tall house or big, the Wupatki Ruin is remarkably well preserved after centuries of exposure to the elements. This

A winter fog envelopes the ruins of Wupatki.

is somehow appropriate in a land that seems timeless—appropriate but unusual. Violent rains arrive each summer, extreme shifts between freeze and thaw happen each winter with often severe winds during the spring and fall. Most of the well-known ruins in the Southwest are found tucked into large rock shelters that give protection from the weather. Wupatki is in the open. Even so, rain often evaporates before it hits the ground so normally perishable material has been preserved. Archeologists and early pothunters have found feathers, cotton clothing, wooden implements and even naturally mummified bodies.

Wupatki was a turning point for the Sinagua. Here they became a pueblo people and remained so even after they left the area. For us Wupatki represents the past, but for the Sinagua it was the future.

The black sand country is rich in archeology but short on water. One of the few dependable sources is the Little Colorado River (above) *that once ran year-around. The plants that thrive here are adapted to the harsh conditions, like the drought-resistant yucca* (right).

The Navajos entered the Wupatki Basin centuries after the pueblos were deserted and many lived in hogans (above).

34

DONEY MOUNTAIN

Elevation: 5290 feet

LOST AND SOMETIMES FOUND. Ben Doney came West with the railroad in 1882. Even before the tracks reached Flagstaff, he helped set up the town's first sawmill. He took up a homestead east of the peaks when the railroad boom quieted. Although he was ten miles from Flagstaff he loved to spend the day walking to and from town, refusing all rides. He would take his wagon and outfit, each winter when the stormy weather moved in, and drop down to the warmer country around Wupatki where he would prospect and dig for artifacts. Over the years he gathered a fine collection from the Wupatki ruins that was seen by Dr. Jesse Fewkes before being sold to a collector and all trace of it lost. Doney began guiding archeologists when digging in the ruins became illegal, but his real passion was searching for a lost mine.

Spanish reports during the seventeenth century mentioned a rich mercury mine located by missionaries forty miles west of the Hopi villages in a red hill at the base of a blue mountain. Doney was convinced this description matched the Wupatki area and spent years looking for the Lost Padre Mine. He located many claims and even sank a shaft through the floor of a pit house on the side of Doney Mountain in hopes of finding the mine. As far as we know he never found what he was looking for, although he continued the search for the rest of his life.

The Navajo used to gather feathers from eagle nests on Doney Mountain, known to them as "Red Mountain," and golden eagles still nest there. The mountain is actually four elongated craters that formed along a major fault. To the west the surface rock is the bleached gray of the Kaibab limestone; to the east is the red rock of the Moenkopi Formation. Paralleling the fault north from Doney Mountain are the uplifted layers of the Black Point Monocline. The highway crosses the cliffs of the escarpment formed by the monocline

Golden eagles nest on Doney Mountain, a series of craters on the edge of the Wupatki Basin.

*The broad sweep of Antelope Prairie is dotted
with locoweed in spring. The attractive blossoms
of this plant can be fatally addictive to horses.*

and connects the Wupatki Basin to the high grasslands of Antelope Prairie.

Although they haven't found Doney's lost mine, archeological survey crews working on Antelope Prairie and throughout the monument have turned up something even more important—new information about the people who once lived here. When Bruce Anderson, an archeologist with the National Park Service, first began an archeological survey in 1981 it was thought the monument contained 800 sites. The completed survey in 1987 showed the number of sites in the monument to be close to 2700. Many of these are related in some way to farming which was much more extensive than originally thought.

To survey a particular area the archeologists must walk over every foot of ground. Members of the survey crew carry daypacks containing food, water and field journals and hold in

their hands bright orange pin flags. The crew members begin by spreading out in even intervals and at a word from the crew chief they begin to walk. Moving at a quick pace, the archeologists carefully scan the ground ahead for anything that doesn't fit into the natural landscape—a potsherd, a pile of stones, a design pecked into a cliff face—whatever may give a clue to the people who once lived here. These features are recorded, mapped and inventoried. The crews that surveyed the wide open spaces

*The sinuous pottery applique on this Sinagua
bowl may represent the common gopher snake.
Harmless, its impersonation of a rattlesnake
is so convincing it can appear dangerous.*

of Antelope Prairie found a very high site density of ninety to 100 sites per square mile. Most of these were rock alignments marking old fields or the crumbled walls of small field houses. Occasionally the archeologists came upon something unusual. An old Colt .44, still loaded, was found a few miles away from a Clovis spear point 11,000 years older.

Antelope Prairie is a place name that almost makes sense. Elusive antelope make their home here. However, they are not true antelope. Scientists generally like to be precise, so prefer to call them pronghorns *(Antilocapra americana)*. They are one of the fastest North American mammals. When startled, they will bolt and raise the white fur on the rump in a flash pattern to confuse predators and warn other pronghorns. The pronghorn isn't the only fast blur dashing through the brush. It might be one of the rare roadrunners *(Geococcyx californianus)*. On a cool morning instead of running to get warm, the roadrunner will stand with its back to the sun and its feathers sticking straight up so the morning light can directly warm the underlying black skin. Whether a roadrunner can outsmart a coyote is open to question, but it is very fast and maneuverable. As it chases down its prey, it uses its tail as a rudder to quickly change directions. The roadrunner chases anything small enough to eat, even snakes.

CITADEL
Elevation: **5400** feet

THE OPEN FRONTIER. The most impressive ruin among this cluster of lava-capped mesas lies on a steep-sided butte with a commanding view of the surrounding countryside. Portions of the ruins were originally two stories high, and the pueblo contained about thirty rooms that may have been occupied by as many as sixty people. Terraces built for farming can still be seen on the slope in front. Known as the Citadel, the name implies a defensive site, but its true function can only be guessed.

With many of the ruins in the region there seems to be a castle mentality at work. They are often built in commanding positions on the sheer edge of a canyon or on top of an isolated butte. The walls are thick, the windows are few, the interior doors are low, and entrance seems to have been from the roof. Yet there is little evidence of warfare. They may have situated their homes merely for a good view of their fields and to keep up with what their neighbors were doing.

The smaller Nalakihu Ruin, from a Hopi word meaning "house standing alone," sits at the foot of the Citadel. It was excavated by the Museum of Northern Arizona and Hopi workmen in 1933. What they found came as a surprise. The pueblo contained ten rooms that were burned at the end of the twelfth century and never reoccupied. Inside the rooms were burial pits containing the bones of numerous owls. Even more puzzling was the realization that almost a third of the broken pottery came from large storage jars that had originally been made near Prescott, Arizona 150 miles away. Were these cumbersome pots carried that far for trade, or is this evidence that a group of Indians had migrated into the Wupatki country?

The idea of a dramatic migration of many different peoples into the Wupatki area following the eruption of Sunset Crater caught the imagination of the early archeologists. The first extensive surveys were conducted by Harold S. Colton, director of the Museum of Northern Arizona. He was

The geometric pattern of this petroglyph, pecked into a basalt boulder near the Citadel, is similar to designs woven in prehistoric textiles.

41

fascinated by the possibility that the eruption of Sunset Crater improved farming conditions in the Wupatki Basin enough to cause a land rush of people from tribes throughout northern Arizona. However, as evidence accumulated over the years, the connection between the eruption and mass migrations of people began to weaken. Peter J. Pilles, Coconino National Forest archeologist, believes the simplest explanation is that local populations of Sinagua, Anasazi and some Cohonina gradually shifted into the Wupatki area.

Nalakihu may be an exception. While the ash from Sunset Crater temporarily improved farming conditions, the main reasons for this population shift seem to be unproductive soils on the flanks of the San Francisco Peaks, which had been farmed for centuries, and an increase in rainfall throughout the Southwest. The dynamic change that occurred in the Sinagua society was not so much a response to the local eruption of a volcano, but to conditions that were affecting Indians through-out the region. Pueblo peoples everywhere were experiencing a cultural expansion at this time. What is still unknown is how much contact occurred among these groups. Was Wupatki a prehistoric melting pot? Almost all sites in the area are mixed, showing traits from various cultures. Some archeologists believe that these different peoples had very close relationships with each other and may have intermarried. Others insist that almost all sites in the area are Sinagua. These questions may be answered after further archeological excavation.

LIFE IN A DRY LAND. Next to the Citadel a large, faulted block of bedrock has slipped forming a three-mile long grabben or shallow valley. Canyons cut into the lava-capped sides of this valley form mesas where prehistoric Indians built numerous pueblos. Most of these are simple affairs—a few rooms, perhaps a kiva—but what is surprising is their numbers. They're everywhere, and yet there is no permanent

water anywhere.

No springs have been found in this area, so it seems the primary source of water was what the Indians collected from infrequent rains. Water control and catchment systems are widespread, and even clay-lined reservoirs are occasionally found. During droughts they may have had to rely on the Little Colorado River, ten miles away. Other desert Indians are known to have traveled long distances for their water. At one time the 173 feet-deep Citadel Sink behind the ruins was thought to have been a natural water hole. But studies indicate the sink was formed by the progressive collapse of one of the many earth cracks found in the area and is too porous to hold water.

Animals that live in this desert grasslands have adapted beautifully to the lack of water. During hot weather the blacktail jackrabbit (*Lepus californicus*) will sit in the shade of a bush waiting until nightfall. As it sits, its large erect ears are pointed seventeen degrees from the north horizon at precisely the coolest area of the sky. The ears are full of blood vessels that radiate body heat, cooling the rabbit without loss of water.

Instead of sitting still in the heat of the day, ravens keep cool by staying in motion. Experiments have found that their black feathers provide a good heat shield as long as a light wind continues to blow over them. During hot weather they are often seen soaring while the rest of the land is still and quiet.

Well camouflaged, this blacktail jackrabbit escapes the midday sun.

LOMAKI

Elevation: 5300 feet

BEAUTIFUL HOUSE. Lomaki was named for the fine stonework of its standing walls. The Hopi name means, "beautiful house." Poised on the edge of a collapsed earth crack, the two-story pueblo was built by the Anasazi Indians about A.D. 1192, although a people that archeologists call the Cohonina may have lived here, too. The nine rooms probably housed two to four families. The quarter-mile trail to Lomaki Ruins passes the mouth of Box Canyon which holds water for short periods after a rain. On both sides of the canyon are small ruins thought to have been lived in by one extended family.

The pueblos of the Wupatki region, which have lasted for centuries, were built from native materials using primitive tools. Many of the ruins still show evidence of fine craftsmanship and must have required an intricate knowledge of stone masonry. This knowledge is now a lost art, and without it preserving the ruins has been difficult. For years the National Park Service used cement to keep the walls from collapsing. However, cement can actually deteriorate the surrounding rock. So the Park Service has gone back to using mud, as did the original builders. Lomaki Ruins have been stabilized without resorting to actual reconstruction.

There is substantial evidence that the prehistoric Indians living in the region were trading with outsiders. Pottery, parrots and macaws, copper bells, and shells from the Gulf of California, the Pacific Coast, and even the Gulf of Mexico indicate an extensive system of prehistoric trade. The existence of a trade network implies the local Indians had something to trade for the exotic goods they were acquiring. It may have been as simple as surplus food, another agricultural product like cotton, or high quality stone for making tools. There is too little evidence yet to do more than guess.

Still on their original string, copper bells like these probably came from Mexico. Shells from as far away as the Pacific and the Gulf of Mexico indicate an extensive prehistoric trade network.

EARTH CRACK. A red-tailed hawk slowly drifts on the mild air currents above the ruins of a prehistoric pueblo. As one spiral brings it close to the ground it suddenly disappears into a deep earth crack.

Many of the large pueblos are built near these earth cracks, suggesting that they may have held special importance for the prehistoric Indians who lived here. Occasionally they are surrounded by low stone walls. Many have been explored, but little information has been gathered about how they were used. A few potsherds, a basket, a few human bone fragments, a pile of corncobs are the only remaining clues.

Earth cracks are narrow fissures in the Kaibab limestone and one has been explored to a depth of 500 feet. A foot bone from an extinct species of camel was found at the bottom of another, indicating that it had been open to the surface for at least 20,000 years. An extensive subterranean crack system probably exists, although most would be too small for a person to enter. The earth cracks are not true caves since they are formed by the movement of the earth's crust that is due, at least in part, to local volcanic activity. Earth cracks are closed to entry because of dangerous conditions.

NORTH ENTRANCE

Elevation: 5600 feet

THE EDGE OF THE JUNIPERS. In the distance, too far to hear, the dark rain of a thunderstorm falls on the Painted Desert. The black and red cinder cones of the San Francisco volcanic field border the horizon to the south and west. This high desert of black cinders is scattered with green junipers and only cut by the narrow highway leading deeper into the grasslands. The open beauty of this country holds people at a distance. A few ranches, the monument headquarters, a trading post or two and the rest lies vacant. At a distance this land is pure geology, but up close it becomes archeology. What today seems empty and unlivable is strewn with the ruins and abandoned fields of prehistoric Indians who once lived here on the edge of the junipers.

THE HOUSE OF TRAGEDY. Big Hawk Valley lies on the western boundary of the monument, a few miles south of the highway. It was a frontier in prehistoric times, where three different groups of Indians—the Sinagua, Anasazi and Cohonina—seem to have lived together peacefully. The close contact among these cultures has presented a complicated picture to archeologists. In 1948, to better understand the relationships among the Indians who lived here, Watson Smith and his crew began to excavate a number of these early sites.

The results of that field season confirmed that there was considerable intermingling. All sites, according to Smith, were originally built by the Sinagua who had moved into the area from the south and were later joined by groups of Cohonina from the west. Eventually Anasazi peoples from the northeast moved in with the resident population. These different groups seemed to live together in peace while retaining their own cultural identity.

That people from different cultures can live together peacefully is not surprising. Since the coming of the Spanish, both the Hopi and Navajo Indians are known to have taken in large groups of refugees from other cultures. So the Sinagua, Anasazi and Cohonina could have lived together without serious disruption. But how long did this last?

During the excavation of Three Courts Pueblo the archeologists uncovered the leg of an adult that had been thrown into, or perhaps buried, in the entrance to the main room. They also discovered the crushed skull and bones of a baby. These finds were unexpected since no evidence for violence had been uncovered during earlier excavations. The archeologists then excavated a pueblo that came to be known as the House of Tragedy. Everywhere they dug they found evidence of violent death. Parts of two legs, perhaps torn from a corpse and

A storm breaks over cinder cones forming part of the 3000 square mile San Francisco Volcanic Field.

deliberately broken, had been carelessly thrown into a room. The rest of the body was never located. In a nearby kiva they found the skeleton of a young woman. Her left leg had been wrenched from the socket at, or shortly after, death. The archeologists determined that this had been the work of humans, not animals. "Scattered in utter confusion," wrote Smith, were numerous human bones, including a badly crushed skull, mixed with broken pottery. The long bones had all been broken and hollowed out as if to extract the marrow, and some had been heated. Smith thought that cannibalism was a possibility, but realized the evidence was not conclusive.

The archeologists could offer no final explanation for what they found. The signs of violence they uncovered could have resulted from a raid by nomadic tribes, from strife among the different groups living here, or from their own tribal justice. The reason will probably never be known, but what is apparent is that violent death was somehow linked to the abandonment of these pueblos. The people never returned, the bodies lay unburied.

The House of Tragedy may be an anomaly. The depopulation of the Wupatki area was gradual, and in most cases seems to have been peaceful. No evidence exists for a mass exodus. People left as conditions slowly worsened. The weather may have cooled enough to shorten the growing season while drought intensified and arroyos began to cut deeper. Winds blew away the cinder cover, possibly clogging water sources, and by the mid-1200s trade networks had been disrupted. Archeologists still argue over which of these was the primary reason for the abandonment of the region. What is not disputed is that life in a desert country is precarious. Even a slight shift in the underlying forces of nature can have its effect. And these forces are always shifting—sometimes dramatically in the case of Sunset Crater, but usually slowly, inexorably. The Wupatki region that had flourished for about 150 years returned to what it always had been—a desert frontier used only occasionally by those moving on to somewhere else.

ACKNOWLEDGMENTS

It's a pleasant surprise when so many people go out their way to help with a project of this sort. Among the many who shared their knowledge and experience are: Wayne Landrum, Bruce Anderson, Steve Cinnamon, and Hank (Henry) Jones of the National Park Service; Peter Pilles of the U.S. Forest Service; Eugene Shoemaker of the U.S. Geological Survey; Bob Cootey of the Museum of Northern Arizona; Arthur Nolan, Pentax Corporation; the Arizona-Sonora Desert Museum; and Christina Watkins.

— S. Thybony, G. Huey

PUBLISHED BY Western National Parks Association

The net proceeds from WNPA publications support educational and research programs in the national parks.

Receive a free Western National Parks Association catalog, featuring hundreds of publications. Email: info@wnpa.org or visit www.wnpa.org

ISBN 0-911-408-67-3

ISBN 978-0-911-408-67-3

WRITTEN BY Scott Thybony

EDITED BY T.J. Preihs

DESIGNED BY Christina Watkins

PHOTOGRAPHY BY George H. H. Huey, except: page 8 (*tree rings*): courtesy of the Laboratory of Tree-Ring Research, University of Arizona; page 9 (*Brady*): courtesy of the Museum of Northern Arizona; page 17: courtesy of the U.S. Geological Survey; page 29: courtesy of the National Park Service; page 34: courtesy of the Museum of Northern Arizona.

MAP BY Eureka Cartography

PRINTING BY Four Colour Imports, Ltd.

PRINTED IN China